DISCARDED
from the Nashville Public Library

D1710210

TOP YOUTUBE STARS™

RACHEL LEVIN

Beauty and Life Hacks Icon with More Than
3 BILLION VIEWS

ANITA LOUISE MCCORMICK

Nashville Public Library

rosen publishing's
rosen central®

New York

Published in 2020 by The Rosen Publishing Group, Inc.
29 East 21st Street, New York, NY 10010

Copyright © 2020 by The Rosen Publishing Group, Inc.

First Edition

All rights reserved. No part of this book may be reproduced in any form
without permission in writing from the publisher, except by a reviewer.

Library of Congress Cataloging-in-Publication Data

Names: McCormick, Anita Louise, author.
Title: Rachel Levin : beauty and life hacks icon with more than 3 billion views
/ Anita Louise McCormick.
Description: First edition. | New York : Rosen Publishing, 2020. | Series: Top
YouTube stars | Includes bibliographical references and index.
Identifiers: LCCN 2019014047| ISBN 9781725348295 (library bound) |
ISBN 9781725348288 (pbk.)
Subjects: LCSH: Levin, Rachel, 1995– | Internet personali-
ties—United States—Biography—Juvenile literature. | YouTube
(Electronic resource)—Biography—Juvenile literature.
Classification: LCC PN1992.9236.L48 M33 2019 | DDC 791.092 [B]—dc23
LC record available at https://lccn.loc.gov/2019014047

Manufactured in the United States of America

On the cover: YouTube star Rachel Levin attends the 7th Annual VidCon
in Anaheim, California. VidCons are conventions where YouTube creators,
advertisers, and fans come to interact.

CONTENTS

When most people decide they want a new color of makeup, they head for the cosmetic aisle of their local store. But when YouTube superstar Rachel Levin decides that she wants a new color of lipstick, she is just as likely to go to the candy store.

Rachel Levin is a top YouTube beauty and fashion guru who's famous for her do-it-yourself (DIY) makeup videos. She creates makeup from all kinds of weird ingredients on her YouTube channel, Rclbeauty101. In her videos, she shows fans how to make lipstick from ingredients such as bubble gum, cotton candy, or even lollypops. She makes face masks out of school glue and glitter and eye liner out of colored pencils. Levin presents her ideas for creating homemade beauty products in a fun way that encourages viewers to try their own beauty product experiments.

Even though YouTube is filled with beauty and fashion videos, Levin's fans agree that her videos are special. Jenny Graham, writer for *Suburban Life* magazine, says, "With so many videos around the Internet, though, it can be difficult to stand out. Yet RCLBeauty101 has a large, dedicated fan base of subscribers that continues to grow by the day, with its popularity skyrocketing since its inception."

Rachel Levin's YouTube channel has been featured in magazines such as *Adweek, Forbes*, and *Cosmopolitan*. That's understandable because her YouTube channel has more than 14 million subscribers. She also has 3.5 million followers on both Instagram and Twitter. Levin's fans even have a special name for themselves: Levinators.

When she started her YouTube channel, nearly all of Levin's videos were makeup and fashion tutorials. But within a few years, Levin decided to expand. She posted comedy skits, life hacks, DIY projects, birthday swaps,

Rachel Levin is a YouTube star who stands out from the crowd. Her down-to-earth style and unique content keep fans coming back to her YouTube channel.

back-to-school tips, and cosplay videos of herself and her friends dressed as Disney princesses, superheroes, and other popular characters.

Levin's astounding variety of videos has inspired other YouTube vloggers to add different types of content to their channels. In a 2018 interview with Tom Ward of *Forbes* magazine, Levin said, "When I did comedy, there were like a ton of beauty gurus and lifestyle people who never did comedy. But the fact that I did comedy; I think that was a way to inspire them to do comedy. Now, every time you see a beauty guru, you see them doing comedy sketches."

Rachel Levin is down-to-earth and funny. Her creativity and sense of fun is amazing. She has collaborated with other YouTubers, including Lilly Singh. Throughout her career, Levin has managed to avoid the drama and controversy that some YouTube vloggers have found themselves involved in. She even avoids swearing. Instead, Levin keeps her channel fun and entertaining. When you watch her channel, she will very likely surprise you with what she comes up with next!

CHAPTER ONE

Growing Up in Philadelphia

Rachel Claire Levin was born in Philadelphia, Pennsylvania, on February 24, 1995. Her father is a doctor and her mother is a lawyer. Levin has three siblings and two stepsiblings. She and her brothers and sisters grew up in a middle-class Philadelphia neighborhood.

EARLY YEARS

Even when Rachel was a young child, she liked to do things her own way. Many children's first word is "mama" or "dada." But

Philadelphia, Pennsylvania, is where Rachel Levin grew up. Philadelphia has a population of more than one and a half million people and is the largest city in Pennsylvania.

Rachel Levin has always loved animals. When she was growing up, she thought about pursuing a career as a veterinarian.

Rachel's first word was "lipstick"! So it was not surprising that she would grow up to have one of the most popular beauty and fashion channels on YouTube. Rachel also got an early start at speaking in complete sentences. Her parents told her that when she was just nine months old, she was putting strings of words together into lengthy sentences. Of course, Rachel's love for talking and expressing herself came in handy when she decided to have a career on YouTube.

Just because "lipstick" was Rachel's first word did not mean that her only interests were makeup and fashion. It might surprise some of her viewers, but when she was growing up, Rachel was somewhat of a tomboy. She liked to roughhouse with her brothers. Sometimes, she liked to play pranks on her brothers and sisters. You can't tell it by looking at her today, but with all that roughhousing, Rachel broke her nose six times as a child.

While Rachel enjoyed the games and activities that often come with being part of a large family, sometimes she needed quiet time to herself. When she wanted to get away from everyone and relax, she climbed up in a tree and sat on a branch.

SWIMMING AND GYMNASTICS

Rachel always loved to be active. She learned to swim when she was two years old. When Rachel was three years old, she discovered that she also enjoyed the challenge of doing gymnastics. Being involved with gymnastics gave Rachel something to focus her energy on. It was fun for her to learn new gymnastic moves and perform them for others.

WRITING

When Rachel was in elementary school, she loved to write. By the time she was in fourth grade, she took on the ambitious project of writing a chapter book. The story was about a mouse and a genie. Her love of writing continued to grow as she went through school. Her love and talent for writing came in handy when she decided to write skits to perform on her YouTube channel.

TEENAGE YEARS BRING CHANGES

Rachel was a bit of a tomboy as a child. But as a teenager, she became more of a "girly girl" and was very interested in makeup and fashion. As a student at Lower Merion High School, Rachel joined the cheerleading team. Like gymnastics, cheerleading

Rachel Levin graduated from Lower Merion High School in Ardmore, Pennsylvania, a suburb of Philadelphia. When she was a student there, she discovered her interest in video production.

was a good outlet for her energy. It also gave her the opportunity to have fun performing for an audience.

ACTING, WRITING, AND VIDEO MAKING

Rachel had interests that went beyond gymnastics and cheerleading. During her middle school and high school years, she loved to write, as well as act in plays and skits. When she was in high school, Rachel took a class where she learned how to record and edit videos in video production classes. When a local Pennsylvania publication, *Suburban Life* magazine, sent writer Jenny Graham to interview Rachel about her YouTube channel in 2014, she wanted

INTERNET SAFETY

The internet is a great place to explore your interests and meet new friends. But it is important to be careful. People on the internet are not always who they say they are. Adults who want to prey on children and teens may pretend to be their age and have similar interests to gain their trust. Because of this, it is important not to give out personal information to people you do not know. And definitely never agree to meet anyone in person whom you know only through the internet unless your parents are present.

If people you meet on the internet insist that you give out personal information, do not answer them. Instead, let your parents know. They can help you decide what to do. They might decide to contact the social media platform and tell them to block this person from contacting you. If the problem is serious enough, they can have law enforcement investigate.

everyone to know how grateful she was to have the opportunity to learn these valuable skills that made her YouTube career possible.

A YOUTUBE FAN

As a teenager, Rachel was a big fan of YouTube. Every day when she came home from school, she turned on her computer and watched the YouTube channels she enjoyed. Her absolute favorites were beauty and fashion videos. She enjoyed watching YouTube vloggers put on makeup and do their hair in different styles. She also loved to watch videos about teen fashion and began to experiment with creating her own look.

CHAPTER TWO

Getting a Start on YouTube

As a teenager, Rachel watched makeup and beauty videos nearly every day. As she put her makeup on, she talked her way through each step, just like the girls in the videos. Rachel told Elizabeth Wellington, fashion writer for the *Philadelphia Inquirer*, "I used to watch a lot of beauty videos on YouTube, and whenever I did my makeup in the mornings, I would do my own tutorials in the mirror."

A LIFE-CHANGING DECISION

Then on December 15, 2010, while she was still in high school, Rachel made a decision that would change her life. She decided to make her own beauty video! Her first video was about how to use concealer to cover under-eye circles. While she didn't have fancy recording equipment like some YouTubers she watched, she thought that it would be a fun project. In her video, Rachel demonstrated how to use CoverGirl's

Simply Ageless concealer. When she finished recording, she signed up for an account on YouTube and posted it.

Rachel did not tell anyone at school about the video. She did not want other students to tease her about it. Soon, people who watched YouTube makeup tutorials started to find Rachel's video. To Rachel's surprise, her video had 457 views in only two days! The fact that people she did not even know were watching encouraged Rachel to make more videos.

Besides makeup and fashion, Rachel has always loved do-it-yourself projects. She did not have a big enough budget to buy expensive department store makeup. So instead of begging her parents for money, she decided to use her love of experimenting to make her own. She found ways to create makeup from things she had around the

Rachel Levin's face is familiar to millions of YouTube viewers. Ever since she made her first video in 2010, she has used her face for all sorts of makeup experiments.

house. She also used inexpensive makeup and mixed it with other ingredients. As she continued to experiment, she was surprised at how many different kinds of makeup she was able to create, from her lipstick made from bubble gum to face masks made from school glue.

BULLYING

Bullying is a very serious problem. Many children and teenagers are bullied at some point in their lives. Some bullying happens in person, but it also happens online. This is called cyberbullying. Online bullying is a difficult challenge because it can take many forms. Some online bullies follow their victims around on social media and harass them. Other times, bullies send hateful texts or email messages. Sometimes, bullies identify themselves. Other times, they use fake identities.

Bullying is a serious problem many teens face. Whether bullying is done in person or online, it can have a negative impact on the victim's life.

Youth who are being bullied can often block a bully on social media platforms, such as Facebook. But that doesn't always solve the problem because even if bullies cannot see what their victims are doing online, they might continue to write untrue and insulting comments about them.

According to Stopbullying.gov, in 2017, 28 percent of youth in grades six to twelve and 20 percent of students in grades nine to twelve reported that they have been bullied. In a survey, 30 percent of youth who responded admitted that they have bullied other students. In 2015, the National Center for Education Statistics and Bureau of Justice Statistics found that 15 percent of high school students have been the victim of cyberbullying.

As time went by, Rachel continued to come up with ideas, then make videos and post them on her YouTube channel. As the number of videos on the channel grew, she started to gain more of a following. Rachel was excited to see that people were not only watching her videos, but they were also subscribing to her channel.

BULLIES AT SCHOOL

As much as she loved to talk as a child, when Rachel entered high school, she started to become shy about speaking up in class. That is because there were bullies in her high school. She

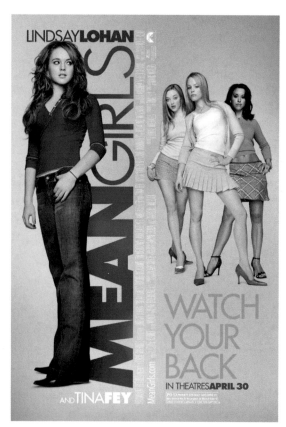

Mean Girls is a 2004 movie about a group of girls who decide to bully other students at their high school.

saw what happened to students the bullies decided to pick on. So she kept quiet to avoid getting their attention.

BULLIES FIND RACHEL'S VIDEOS

Rachel was not the only person at her school who watched beauty and fashion videos on YouTube; it was a popular activity for many teenage girls. One day, a girl from Rachel's school came across her video channel. She not only watched her videos, but she showed them to other students.

In a 2018 interview with *Forbes* magazine writer Tom Ward, Levin recalled what happened after that. "When I was 15 and they found out about my YouTube ... picture *Mean Girls*, when she walked into school and everyone stared at her. That's what happened when they all found out about YouTube."

The bullies were jealous and did not want Rachel to be popular. They took every opportunity to tease her. This made Rachel very upset. At one point, Rachel seriously considered taking her videos down so the girls would stop teasing her.

But after she thought about it, Rachel decided not to let the bullies defeat her. She loved making and posting videos, and the bullies would probably continue to tease her even if she deleted her channel. So Rachel continued to create videos about makeup, fashion, and other things she enjoyed. The more videos Rachel posted, the more her fan base grew.

YOUTUBE AS A CAREER

While Rachel was still in high school, she decided that she enjoyed making videos so much that she wanted to do it as a career. By making videos, she could do several things she enjoyed, including writing, acting, and editing. Rachel knew that some YouTube stars made a living by creating and posting videos, and she wanted to do that, too.

Like most schools, Rachel's high school had a guidance counselor who met with students to help them plan for their future. When Rachel met with the school guidance counselor, she said that she really wanted to have a career making videos and being a YouTube vlogger. Rachel hoped that the guidance counselor would give her some advice on how to make that happen, but instead the guidance counselor recommended that Rachel choose another career.

Rachel refused to be discouraged. She loved making videos too much to give up on her dream career. So she continued to create and post videos, and her audience continued to grow.

CHAPTER THREE

Rachel's YouTube Channel Grows

As Rachel's following on YouTube grew, she decided to be more creative with her videos. Her channel still had mostly beauty and fashion tutorials, but in addition to the make-up tutorials, she started posting funny videos about how she created her own makeup. She also posted life hacks and back-to-school tips, as well as videos on other topics.

THE *WALL STREET JOURNAL* NOTICES RCLBEAUTY101

In September 2011, when Rachel was sixteen years old, she got a major break. Her YouTube channel was featured along with other YouTube beauty gurus in the *Wall Street Journal* article by Alina Dizik "Mixing Makeup for the Webcam."

The exposure that resulted gave her many new viewers, and more advertisers became interested in reaching her audience.

FANS GET TO MEET LEVIN'S FAMILY

Since some of Levin's videos were about her everyday life, she decided to introduce her family to her fans. Levin's sister Daniella has been in some of her videos. In 2014, Levin brought her mother in front of the camera for a YouTube Mom Tag video.

In 2013, Levin started dating Isaac Nakash. Soon, Levin decided to introduce Nakash to her YouTube fans. While they were dating, he appeared in some of Levin's videos. Inspired by Levin, Nakash started his own YouTube channel, IsaacLive, that focuses on pranking others, stunts, and funny skits.

Penn State Brandywine is a campus of Pennsylvania State University. The school is located in Middletown Township, Pennsylvania, and has approximately 1,700 students.

GOING TO PENN STATE

In 2013, Levin started college at Penn State Brandywine, where she planned to major in communications. But during her first year of college, she discovered how difficult it was to be a full-time college student and continue to make videos for her YouTube channel. Levin wanted to make sure that her videos looked as good as possible. She sometimes spends up to seventeen hours filming and editing a six-minute video. So after her first year at Penn State, Levin made a decision to focus on her YouTube career instead of going back to college.

FIVE HUNDRED THOUSAND SUBSCRIBERS

By August 2014, Levin's YouTube channel had five hundred thousand subscribers. To celebrate this milestone with her fans, she announced that she would host a 500K Subscriber Giveaway. The prizes included a MacBook Pro, an iPad, and a GoPro. News of the big giveaway brought even more subscribers to her YouTube channel.

That month, Levin decided to make a video of a comedy skit she wrote called "Back to School – Expectations vs Reality." The video proved to be popular, so Levin continued writing and making more comedy videos.

By September 2014, Levin's YouTube channel, Rclbeauty101 had six hundred thousand subscribers. That was an additional one hundred thousand subscribers in only a month.

CAREERS IN VIDEO PRODUCTION

While it is fun to create and post videos, not everyone who starts a YouTube channel will become a YouTube star and social media influencer. As with actors, people who play sports, singers, and musicians, only a small percentage of people who have YouTube channels can attract enough of an audience to make a living at it. Currently, YouTube will not allow people to monetize, or run advertising on their YouTube channel, unless they have at least one thousand subscribers. With so many channels on YouTube, it usually takes quite a while to reach that number of subscribers before vloggers can make any profit.

There are still many ways to make a living in video production. Video careers that do not involve YouTube can be fun, challenging, and exciting. Many television stations hire people to make and edit videos. In addition to that, videos are an important part of many businesses' social media. Advertising agencies also hire people to make videos for their clients. There are many good books on the market with information on video careers.

It is also possible to have a freelance career or a side job making and editing videos. That way, you can schedule your own hours and pick clients that are the best fit for your interests and skills.

Meanwhile, making and posting videos on YouTube can give you valuable experience you can use later on if you decide to pursue a career in video.

HIRING A MANAGER

As Levin became more popular, she realized that she needed help with the business end of her career. Planning, filming, and editing videos took a lot of time. Levin did not want to have to spend time sorting through offers, planning events, and so on. She also wanted someone who could help her negotiate contracts, so she decided to hire Naomi Lennon, of Lennon Management in Los Angeles, a manager who worked with several YouTube vloggers.

Hiring a manager proved to be a good decision for Levin. Now that she no longer had to focus on business, Levin had more time to focus on the creative side of things. Having a manager also helped Levin to negotiate better deals with companies that wanted her to promote their products and services on YouTube and her other social media channels.

CHAPTER FOUR

Success as a Social Media Influencer

In 2015, Levin's YouTube channel Rclbeauty101 had one million subscribers! Levin wanted to do something to thank her fans for their loyalty, so she celebrated by having a big YouTube giveaway party for her fans. Levin told Elizabeth Wellington from the *Daily Gazette*, "I never thought I would ever be that popular. I'm shocked every single day."

Because of her large following, Levin was starting to be known as a social media influencer. That means that her presence on social media platforms, such as YouTube, Instagram, and Twitter, was attracting a significant number of people. In 2015, Zefr, a company that creates targeted

Due to the popularity of her YouTube channel, Rachel Levin has been nominated in multiple categories for the Teen Choice Award and the Streamy Award.

23

video ad placements, ranked Levin as the top social media influencer under twenty-one.

TEEN CHOICE AND STREAMY AWARDS

In 2015, Levin was nominated for a Teen Choice Award and a Streamy Award. The Teen Choice Awards honor celebrities in all fields of entertainment. Teens vote for the winners through social media sites. The Streamy Awards recognize and honor people who are involved in all areas of online videos. Just like the Academy Awards, the Streamy Awards offer recognition in many categories, including video writing, acting, and directing.

BEING A POSITIVE INFLUENCE

This new role as a social media influencer helped Levin to earn a higher income through her YouTube channel. Because of Rclbeauty101's rapid growth, more companies started seeking Levin out to promote their products and services to her fans. It also caused Levin to think about ways that she could be a more positive influence and role model to her fans.

In 2015, Levin appeared in a video with other teen celebrities to warn viewers against the dangers of smoking. The video, titled "It's a Trap!," emphasized that even occasional social smoking at parties, on the weekend, or just every now and then can get teens hooked on nicotine. The video was produced by Truth Campaign, an organization that works to educate teens about the dangers of smoking and other tobacco use.

TEENS AND BODY IMAGE

In today's world, there is a lot of emphasis on having the perfect body. Television, movies, magazines, and billboard ads are filled with pictures of slim models with perfect-looking skin, hair, and faces. The majority of those models would not look nearly that perfect in person. But the image they project through edited photos have made generations of teens feel unhappy about the way they look.

While body image issues are a minor issue for some, they can cause serious problems for other teens. Being dissatisfied with how they look can cause teens to have a poor self-image and lack of confidence that carries over into all areas of their lives. Some teens feel like they will never look good enough to be popular at school, find a mate, get a good job, or achieve success in other ways. This can cause some teens to go on extreme diets in hopes of losing weight and develop dangerous eating disorders, such as anorexia and bulimia. If left untreated, eating disorders can cause long-term health problems or even death.

ANTIBULLYING VIDEO

Because she had been bullied as a teenager in high school, Levin knew from firsthand experience how difficult life can be when someone in your life decides to bully you. And as a YouTube star, she knows how it feels to read negative comments posted by people she has never met. Sometimes, people who

Rachel Levin takes a selfie while attending Neon Carnival on April 13, 2019, in Thermal, California. The event was sponsored by Levi's.

comment on YouTube videos hide behind the anonymity of their computer to insult vloggers harshly. People who do that often don't think about the fact that they are posting those comments to a real human being.

So Levin decided to make an antibullying video for her viewers. She did this so that any of her viewers who were being bullied would know that they were not alone. She also wanted anyone who watched the video to stop and think about how actions and words affect others, even famous people online that they might never meet in person. The video was titled "Dont Hurt Me." In it, Levin is walking down the hall at school, and other students are insulting her. She sits down and looks at her computer screen. The closing message of the video is, "If you wouldn't say it in person, then why would you say it online?" In the video's description, Levin wrote, "I wanted to make this video to remind everyone that even with all the things going on in the world, you don't have to be part of the problem."

BODY IMAGE VIDEO

Another issue that Levin was concerned about is body image. She was aware that many teens, especially girls, always say negative things about the way their face and body looks. So she thought of creative ways to make a video that would reach her fans.

In 2016, Levin made a video titled "I Am Ugly" to bring attention to the issue and help her teenage viewers be kinder to themselves. In the video, Levin talked to herself in the mirror about everything that people had told her was wrong with her appearance. Then, a younger version of herself appears, and the adult Levin realizes how damaging it can be to hear negative comments about your appearance.

CHAPTER FIVE

Expanding in New Directions

As Levin's fan base continued to grow, she expanded the scope of her video channel. She wrote new kinds of comedy skits and acted them out with her friends in front of the video camera. She created videos about topics that had been

Rachel Levin enjoys swapping birthday gifts with YouTube vloggers. It is a fun way for Rachel to share her birthday surprises with viewers.

popular previously on her channel, including life hacks and going back to school. She even asked her fans what they would like to see her make videos about.

NEW KINDS OF VIDEOS

One fun activity Levin enjoys doing are birthday swaps. She connects with YouTuber vloggers who celebrate a birthday in the same month as her. Then they set a spending limit and send each other a box of gifts. When the gift boxes arrive, both YouTubers make videos of themselves opening the packages.

Once Rachel Levin discovered that her fans love Disney princesses, she made several videos with her and her friends dressing up in Disney princess costumes.

Like many teens and young adults, Levin found that she enjoyed dressing up and doing cosplay. So she decided to incorporate cosplay costumes in some of her comedy skits. Levin and her friends dressed as Disney princesses in some videos and as superheroes in others.

All those costumes cost a lot of money. But the increased revenue Levin was earning from YouTube advertising, as well as the money she earned from working with sponsors, made it possible for her to create videos that were more expensive to produce. This was especially true of the Disney Princess Pool Party videos, which required renting several costumes and a mansion with a pool.

However, the investment paid off. The first Disney Princess Pool Party video was so popular that Levin and her friends made an entire series of videos, including Disney Princess Birthday Party, Disney Princess Prom, Disney Princess Date Night, Disney Princess Last Day of School, Disney Princess Slumber Party, and Disney Princess Carpool Ride.

FANS WANT TO KNOW EVERYTHING!

Levin has always enjoyed making videos about things that are going on in her life. She likes to talk about activities she enjoys, products she likes, and people in her life. But as a YouTube celebrity vlogger, Levin has also learned that decisions she makes in her personal life sometimes affect her fans.

Breaking up with a boyfriend is a common thing in most teenagers' and young adults' lives. But when it happens to a popular YouTube star, it can feel like the whole world need to know all about it.

In November 2016, after being together for three years, Levin and her boyfriend, Isaac Nakash, mutually decided to break up. Some fans were heartbroken because they enjoyed seeing Nakash in Levin's videos and enjoyed watching their relationship grow.

Rachel Levin and her boyfriend, Tyler Regan, enjoy making public appearances together. Regan has his own YouTube channel and sometimes collaborates with Levin to make videos.

Several months after the breakup, Levin started dating Tyler Regan. Regan also had a YouTube channel, and they soon started making videos together. When Levin introduced her new boyfriend to her fans in April 2017, many viewers were happy for her, but others told her she should drop her new boyfriend and go back to Nakash. These fans had never met Levin or Nakash, yet they felt like they knew her from watching her videos.

Levin reassured her fans that she was very happy with her new boyfriend. But some fans were still upset. In a November 2016 post on Twitter, Levin tried explaining it to her fans again. She posted, "For everyone that's been asking about my relationship. I'm sorry if this upsets you but I love you guys so much & hope you understand."

COSPLAY

"Cosplay" is short for "costume play." Actors who perform in plays have been dressing up as characters for thousands of years. However, cosplay is a relatively new idea.

Being involved with cosplay is very different from acting in plays, movies, or television shows. Instead of memorizing a script, as actors do, people who participate in cosplay dress up as characters they like just to have fun. These characters can be from movies, television shows, video games, books, or comics. Most characters people cosplay are from pop culture. Cosplay is often part of comic, science fiction, or other conventions that celebrate pop culture.

Cosplay is a fun and popular way for people to dress up as characters they like. Many cosplayers enjoy getting together at meet-ups and conventions.

Some cosplayers order costumes that are ready to wear. Others enjoy the challenge of making their own costumes. Some cosplayers enjoy making costumes so much that they run a business making them for others who do not have the time or skill to make their own.

Some cosplay enthusiasts go to national, regional, or local conventions where people get together to share their interest in this fun activity.

NATIONAL TV APPEARANCES

By 2015, national television show producers started to take notice of Levin's growing popularity. In October 2015, Levin appeared on *Today*. She joined Tamron Hall to share creepy DIY Halloween craft ideas with their audience. Levin's DIY projects included eyeball candy and glow-in-the-dark trick-or-treat bags.

In 2016, Steve Harvey invited her to appear on his show to give advice to YouTube vloggers who wanted to gain more subscribers and expand their audience.

These television appearances and other media interviews undoubtedly brought new fans to Levin's channel. They provided media exposure beyond YouTube and other social media outlets and introduced Levin and her unique brand to people who might not have even thought about watching YouTube vloggers.

CHAPTER SIX

Looking Toward the Future

As Levin's fan base has grown, she has continued to find ways to connect with her viewers. This is a very important skill for a YouTube vlogger to have, and Levin has

Rachel Levin speaks at a social media influencer panel at a 2018 Glendale, California, fashion and beauty conference. Because of her large number of followers, many companies have worked with her to promote their products and services.

managed to do this better than most. She updates her You-Tube, Instagram, Twitter, and Snapchat content on a regular basis and always keeps it fun and interesting. As her interests change and expand, her content on social media develops right along with it.

SOCIAL MEDIA INFLUENCERS

When YouTube vloggers gain a large-enough audience, they become what the advertising world now calls a social media influencer. A social media influencer is someone with a social media platform, such as YouTube, who has enough of a following to influence the buying decisions their viewers make.

In the past, advertisers who wanted to reach teens and young adults planned much of their marketing around ad campaigns in magazines, radio, and television. Most advertisers still connect with young consumers though major media outlets. But after the rise of YouTube stars, many companies that want to reach young audiences go to social media influencers to get the word out about their products and services.

Advertisers have found that working with social media influencers is different from the ad campaigns of the past. When social media influencers promote a product, they rarely read directly from a script. Instead, they often find ways to talk about the product or service that will sound genuine to their audience.

This approach means that advertisers who want to work with social media influencers usually have to give up some control. But in exchange for that, they are able to reach viewers who might never see the ads they run in other media outlets.

KEEPING VIEWERS

Sometimes when YouTubers get beyond the age of the teenage audience that watched when they started, their audience starts to decrease. This often happens because the YouTubers are no longer in touch with the world their viewers live in. But this has not happened to Levin.

Even though Levin is now an adult and no longer in school, she has found ways to create videos that appeal to her current fans and attract new viewers.

Instead of just doing videos about makeup and life at school, Levin has taken on new topics, such as dating, cosplay, and other activities that interest a wide range of viewers. As Levin has done this, her YouTube channel continues to grow. In early 2019, her YouTube channel hit fourteen million subscribers.

Levin's fans appreciate her funny and honest down-to-earth approach to life and her innovative ways of making videos. It is what keeps them coming back.

CREATIVE FREEDOM

Levin shows her creativity in all aspects of her career. When she works with advertisers, Levin likes to use her own creativity to present the product or service instead of reading a script. Brands such as the retail chain Target and Birchbox, a service that delivers top brands of makeup, have sought Levin out and worked with her to promote their businesses.

In an interview with Hannah Li of Digiday, Levin described how she likes to work with advertisers. She said, "What I find most effective when I work with brands personally is when

STARTING YOUR OWN YOUTUBE CHANNEL

So you have decided to start your own YouTube channel. Congratulations! It doesn't cost anything to have a channel on YouTube, and the experiences you'll have making and posting videos can be amazing.

Before you start a channel, think about the kind of videos you want to make. It might be the kind of videos you like to watch. In the beginning at least, it's a good idea to keep your videos on one topic. That way, if viewers like one video they watch, they will be likely to come back to see more.

Some YouTube vloggers record their videos and then edit them before posting. Other vloggers live-stream on YouTube. Some do both. The choice is yours!

There are many how-to videos and books available about how to start a channel on YouTube that offer great suggestions for beginners. You might also find classes in your area.

When you are making videos for YouTube, always keep internet safety in mind. When you post a channel, you do not have to use your full name. You might want to just use your first name and then call your channel something that has to do with the topic of your videos. Or you might decide to use a name you make up. If you are not sure how much information you should give out in your videos, it's a good idea to talk to your parents and see what advice they offer.

The YouTube rules say that you have to be at least thirteen years old to have a channel. If you are under thirteen, you can ask your parents to set up an account.

they give me the creative freedom to do what I know best with my channel."

When Birchbox decided to partner with Levin, they allowed her to use her own creative ideas to present their company to her viewers. Instead of making a commercial, Levin worked Birchbox into a video she made about going to the Coachella Music Festival. She called the video "How Girls Act at Coachella" and included scenes where she used Birchbox products to touch up her makeup while she was at the music festival. Birchbox was very pleased with Levin's ideas.

WHAT THE FUTURE HOLDS

Whatever directions Levin's career might take in the future, her ability to connect with her fans and deliver content they love is sure to keep her YouTube channel active and growing.

In an interview with Elizabeth Wellington, fashion writer for the *Philadelphia Inquirer*, Levin said, "I didn't think it was possible for me to have the life I have right now. And if I have so much happiness right now, I'm excited to see what the future holds."

And so do more than fourteen million of her fans!

TIMELINE

- **1995** Rachel Claire Levin is born in Philadelphia, Pennsylvania.
- **2010** Levin posts her first video on YouTube.
- **2011** Levin's YouTube channel, Rclbeauty101, is featured in a *Wall Street Journal* article, "Mixing Makeup for the Webcam."
- **2013** Levin begins dating Isaac Nakash.
- **2014** Levin holds a 500K Subscriber Giveaway. During the video, she announces the contest winners.
- **2015** Levin's YouTube channel hits the one million subscriber mark. In August, Rclbeauty101 becomes the fastest-growing YouTube channel in the world. Levin is nominated for a Teen Choice Award. Levin participates in an antismoking video, "It's a Trap." Levin also appear on *Today* to share do-it-yourself ideas for Halloween.
- **2016** *The Steve Harvey Show* invites Levin to come and advise YouTube vloggers on how to attract more subscribers. Levin posts one of her most popular videos of all time, "Disney Princess Pool Party." She also posts a video titled "I Am Ugly" about teens and self-image.
- **2017** Levin posts a video to bring awareness to the harm done by bullying titled "Dont Hurt Me."
- **2019** Rclbeauty101 reaches the fourteen million subscriber mark.

GLOSSARY

brands Companies that sell products or services.

collaborate To work with other people toward a common goal.

cosplay Dressing up as a character from TV, movies, or books and acting out that character's role.

cyberbullying Bullying that is done over the internet or through texting or other forms of messaging.

followers People who track someone's posts on YouTube or other social media websites.

gymnastics A sport in which athletes demonstrate strength, balance, and body control.

influencer A person who has a large social media following and can influence others to buy products or services.

life hacks Hints on how people can do things to make their everyday lives easier or more efficient.

manager A person who takes care of the business dealings of an entertainer or YouTube star.

monetize To earn money from doing something, such as running ads on a video channel.

role model A person whom others respect and look up to.

social media Websites and apps that allow users to create content and share it with others.

social media platforms Websites or other social media applications, such as YouTube, Instagram, and Twitter, where people can share content.

sponsor A business that provides funding for an activity, usually in exchange for advertising.

subscribers People who are on a list to automatically receive updates from people, organizations, or businesses that post on social media.

vlog A video blog, such as a YouTube channel.

vlogger A person who posts video blogs, especially on YouTube.

FOR MORE INFORMATION

Bullying Canada
471 Smythe Street
PO Box 27009
Fredericton, NB E3B 9M1
Canada
(877) 352-4497
Website: http://
    www.bullyingcanada.ca
Facebook and Twitter:
    @BullyingCanada
Bullying Canada provides
    resources to assist victims of
    in-person and online bullying.

Futurpreneur Canada
133 Richmond Street West,
    Suite 700
Toronto, ON M5H 2L3
Canada
(866) 646-2922
Website: https://www
    .futurpreneur.ca/en
Facebook and Instagram:
    @futurpreneur
This program offers assistance
    to young Canadians to start
    a business.

National Costumers
    Association
PO Box 3406
Englewood, CO 80155
(303) 339-0750
Website: https://www
    .costumers.org
Facebook: @NATLCostumers
Instagram: @national
    costumersassociation
This organization promotes and
    preserves the artistic and his-
    torical aspects of costuming.

National Youth Internet Safety
    and Cyberbullying Task
    Force, Inc.
1850 Riverfront Center
Amsterdam, NY 12010-4621
(844) 767-4722
Website: https://www
    .nationalyouthiscbtaskforce
    .org
Facebook:
    @nationalyouthiscbtaskforce
This task force educates youth
    about cyberbullying.

PACER's National Bullying Prevention Center
PACER Center, Inc.
8161 Normandale Boulevard
Bloomington, MN 55437
(800) 537-2237
Website: https://www.pacer.org/bullying
Facebook:
@PACERsNational
BullyingPreventionCenter
Instagram and Twitter:
@PACER_NBPC
PACER provides educational materials about bullying for use by teachers or students.

Project Fashion
Experience America
4556 University Way NE, Suite 200
Seattle, WA 98105
(800) 410-6088
Website: https://fashion.experienceamerica.com
Facebook: @projectfashionla
Project Fashion operates the Experience America summer program to give students hands-on experience in the fashion and design industry.

Truth Initiative
900 G Street NW, Fourth Floor
Washington, DC 20001
(202) 454-5555
Website: https://truthinitiative.org
Facebook and Twitter:
@truthinitiative
Truth Initiative works to educate the public about the dangers of smoking and other tobacco use.

Young Entrepreneur Council (YEC)
745 Atlantic Avenue
Boston, MA 02110
(484) 403-0736
Website: https://yec.co
Facebook: @yecorg
Instagram: @YEC
YEC works to help the next generation of entrepreneurs. People who are interested can apply for an invitation on the website.

FOR FURTHER READING

Birley, Shane. *How to Be a Blogger and Vlogger in 10 Easy Lessons.* Lake Forest, CA: Walter Foster Jr., 2016.

Furgang, Adam. *20 Great Career-Building Activities Using YouTube.* New York, NY: Rosen Publishing, 2017.

Hall, Kevin. *Creating and Building Your Own YouTube Channel.* New York, NY: Rosen Central, 2017.

Hand, Carol. *Getting Paid to Produce Videos.* New York, NY: Rosen Publishing, 2017.

Kyncl, Robert, and Maany Peyvan. *Streampunks: YouTube and the Rebels Remaking Media.* New York, NY: Harper-Business, 2017.

Loh-Hagan, Virginia. *YouTube Channel.* Ann Arbor, MI: 45th Parallel Press, 2017.

Paul, Harriet, Caroline Rowlands, and Gideon Summerfield. *The Vloggers Yearbook.* New York, NY: Little Bee Books, 2015.

Putnam, Will, and We the Unicorns. *Vlogging 101: The Ultimate Guide to Becoming a YouTuber.* London, UK: Studio Press, 2017.

Roberts, Laura. *Careers in Digital Media,* San Diego, CA: ReferencePoint Press Inc., 2018.

Staley, Erin. *Vloggers and Vlogging.* New York, NY: Rosen Publishing, 2017.

BIBLIOGRAPHY

Adams, Char. "WATCH: Beauty Blogger Rachel Levin Confronts Her Negative Body Image in 'I Am Ugly.'" *People*, September 16, 2016. https://people.com/bodies/beauty-blogger -confronts-negative-body-image-with-youtube-video.

Bryant, Miranda. "A Beauty Blogger Attacks Her Looks in a Powerful New Video." *Daily Mail*, September 16, 2016. http://www.dailymail.co.uk/~/article-3793502/index.html.

Carter, Brooke. "Rachel Levin Net Worth 2018—How Much She Makes Per Video." Gazette Review (blog), August 9, 2017. https://gazettereview.com/2017/08/rachael-levin-net -worth-wealthy-beauty-guru-now.

Dizik, Alina. "Mixing Makeup for the Webcam." *Wall Street Journal*, September 21, 2011. https://www.wsj.com/articles /SB10001424053111904194604576582673307645698.

Graham, Jenny. "Teen Queen." *Suburban Life*, July 2014. http://www.suburbanlifemagazine.com/articles /?articleid=1042.

Gutelle, Sam. "YouTube, Vine Stars on Smoking Cigarettes: 'It's a Trap!'" Tubefilter, August 27, 2015. https://www .tubefilter.com/2015/08/27/truth-anti-smoking-its-a-trap.

Hamedy, Saba. "Who Are the Top Digital Video Influencers Under 21?" Mashable, December 12, 2015. https:// mashable.com/2015/12/12/who-are-the-20-top-digital-video -influencers-under-21/#um.jOwv3xqqt.

Harvey, Steve (Steve TV Show). "How to Become a YouTube Star! || STEVE HARVEY." YouTube, April 16, 2016. https:// www.youtube.com/watch?v=6HYadOvqBsw.

Johnson, Lauren. "After 11 Years in Digital Video, YouTube Wants to Take on TV-Sized Budgets." *Adweek*, May 1, 2016. https://www.adweek.com/digital/after-11-years-digital-video-youtube-wants-take-tv-sized-budgets-171156.

Levin, Rachel (Rclbeauty101). "Dont Hurt Me." YouTube, November 17, 2017. https://www.youtube.com/watch?v=nfbwPTsowEA&feature=youtu.be.

Levin, Rachel (Rclbeauty101). "How Girls Act at Coachella!" YouTube, April 24, 2015. https://www.youtube.com/watch?v=3FiBSvKHfas.

Schiffer, Jessica. "Beauty Influencer Rachel Levin Is Putting a Playful Spin on YouTube Beauty." Glossy, March 9, 2018. https://www.glossy.co/new-face-of-beauty/video-blogger-rachel-levin-is-putting-a-playful-spin-on-youtube-beauty.

Stopbullying.gov. "What Is Cyberbullying." US Department of Health and Human Services, July 26, 2018. https://www.stopbullying.gov/cyberbullying/what-is-it/index.html.

Ward, Tom. "Rachel Levin: A YouTuber with a Positive Message." *Forbes*, January 26, 2018. https://www.forbes.com/sites/tomward/2018/01/26/rachel-levin-a-youtuber-with-a-postive-message.

Wellington, Elizabeth. "At 21, Main Line YouTube Star Rachel Levin Can Move a Product, Pack a Mall." *Inquirer*, June 21, 2016. https://www.philly.com/philly/living/style/20160622_At_21__Main_Line_YouTube_star_Rachel_Levin_can_move_a_product__pack_a_mall.html.

Wellington, Elizabeth. "Just 21, Her Videos Get 100 Million Views a Month." *Daily Gazette*, June 28, 2016. https://dailygazette.com/article/2016/06/28/levin.

Yi, Hannah. "'Give Me the Creative Freedom': YouTube Star Rclbeauty101 on Working with Brands." Digiday, January 19, 2016. https://digiday.com/marketing/brands-rclbeauty101.

INDEX

ABOUT THE AUTHOR

Anita Louise McCormick is the author of many books. Her previous titles for Rosen Publishing include *Tyler Oakley: LGBTQ+ Activist with More Than 660 Million Views* (Top YouTube Stars), *Rosa Parks and the Montgomery Bus Boycott* (Spotlight on the Civil Rights Movement), *The Native American Struggle in United States History*, and *Everything You Need to Know About Nonbinary Gender Identities* (The Need to Know Library).

PHOTO CREDITS

Cover, p. 1 Tara Ziemba/WireImage/Getty Images; p. 5 Robin Marchant/Getty Images; p. 7 Songquan Deng/Shutterstock.com; p. 8 Rachid Ait/Shutterstock; p. 10 Gina Ferazzi/Los Angeles Times/Getty Images; p. 13 Mike Windle/Getty Images; p. 14 Antonio Guillem/Shutterstock.com; p. 16 Moviestore collection Ltd/Alamy Stock Photo; p. 19 Penn State/Flickr/Orchard Hall at Penn State Brandywine/CC BY-NC-ND 2.0; p. 23 Featureflash Photo Agency/Shutterstock.com; p. 26 Tommaso Boddi/Getty Images; p. 28 GCapture/Shutterstock.com; p. 29 Gerardo Mora/WireImage/Getty Images; p. 31 Willy Sanjuan/Invision/AP Images; p. 32 Araya Diaz/WireImage/Getty Images; p. 34 Vivien Killilea/Getty Images.

Design: Michael Moy; Layout: Ellina Litmanovich; Editor: Xina M. Uhl; Photo Researcher: Nicole DiMella